THE
Connection
EXPERIENCE

Get connections working for you

TRICIA SYBERSMA

All rights reserved. No portion of this book may be reproduced mechanically, electronically, or by any other means, including photocopying, without written permission from the author. It is illegal to copy this book, post it to a website, or distribute it by any other means without permission from the author.

HeartMath® is a registered trademark of Quantum Intech, Inc.
For all HeartMath® trademarks go to www.heart.com/trademarks

Ebook ISBN 978-1-948074-70-4
Print ISBN 978-1-948074-68-1

This publication is designed to provide accurate and authoritative information regarding the subject matter covered. It is sold with the understanding that the author is not engaged in rendering professional services. If legal, accounting, medical, psychological, or any other expert assistance is required, seek the services of a competent professional.

Disclaimer: This book does not provide medical advice.
The information, including but not limited to, text, graphics, images and other material contained in this book are for informational purposes. Always seek the advice of a professional health care provider with any questions regarding your medical conditions and treatments.

Cover design and layout rework by Rachel Rossano

Copyright © 2022 by Tricia Sybersma

What's waiting for you

The Experiences Explained
Why the Experiences were created...................4

Welcome to the Connection Experience
My Connection Story.....................................7
What is Connection..9
Getting in the Connection Vibe............................12

Connection to you
Connection to your Physical Body.....................16
Bonus - Quick Coherence.........................18
Connection to your Energy....................................19
Connection to your Unique Perspective........25
Connection to your Inner Power........................34
One Minute Manifest..39
Boundaries 41

Connection to the world around you
Connection to Nature..43
Connection to Community and Beyond.......47
Intro to Navigating...55
Wrapping up with Affirmations..........................60

The Experiences Explained

Who else struggles with an inner dialogue that sounds something like this;

- Why do I feel dissatisfied, bored, and overwhelmed all at the same time?
- Why do I feel stuck in a pattern that has no way out?
- Why do I feel like everything is such an effort?
- How do I begin to change how I feel about myself and my day-to-day life?
- How do I begin to reconnect and trust my instincts?
- How do I begin to enjoy the simple pleasures of everyday life?
- And more...

All too often society teaches us to look outwards for answers. It wasn't until a series of events invited me to look inward that I realized **the way out of my patterns was to go in** and experience the wealth of knowledge and wisdom available just beyond my awareness.

You also have a wealth of knowledge and wisdom just waiting to be discovered in your inner world.

Discover and explore your inner world, so you can change your outer world.

The Experiences were created with simple yet practical suggestions to guide you on your journey of embracing life in the changing world around you.

GRATITUDE

CONNECTION

ACTION

Welcome to The Connection Experience
THE SECOND STEP OF THE GRATITUDE ~ CONNECTION ~ ACTION JOURNEY

I'm delighted you are here. For this experience, I invite you to explore Connections in a profound and powerful way. It seems everyone is talking about Connections. Science is a buzz with studies about how everyone and everything is connected!

Just for a moment, imagine what living in Connection with yourself and the world around you might look like.

You may feel excited or overwhelmed. What if you'd rather not be connected to everyone and everything but have the power to choose the Connections that are right for you?
Yes, it's possible!

Learning about Connections changed how I live my life. It also had a powerful impact on those in my field of Connection. Once you understand how Connections work, you can begin to make powerful changes in your life by choosing the Connections that benefit you.

> " *Like a string of party lights, Connections are energy, and you have the power to turn them on or off.* "
>
> ~ Tricia Sybersma

How The Gratitude Experience complements The Connection Experience

The Gratitude, Connection, Action journey is dynamic.

Gratitude opens Connections, which leads to Action. This, in turn, inspires more Gratitude, opening more Connections and more Action, a process that **creates momentum, expansion, and positive changes in your life.**

The Gratitude Experience offers a fresh, new way of understanding gratitude as a theme and, more importantly, as an energy. You'll learn how to activate gratitude in four key areas.

- Gratitude for your physical body
- Gratitude for the physical world
- Gratitude for how you think and feel
- Gratitude for how you experience your life

Gratitude creates a welcoming environment that nurtures change so it's not scary or intimidating. You can use gratitude as your foundation as you explore your field of Connections.

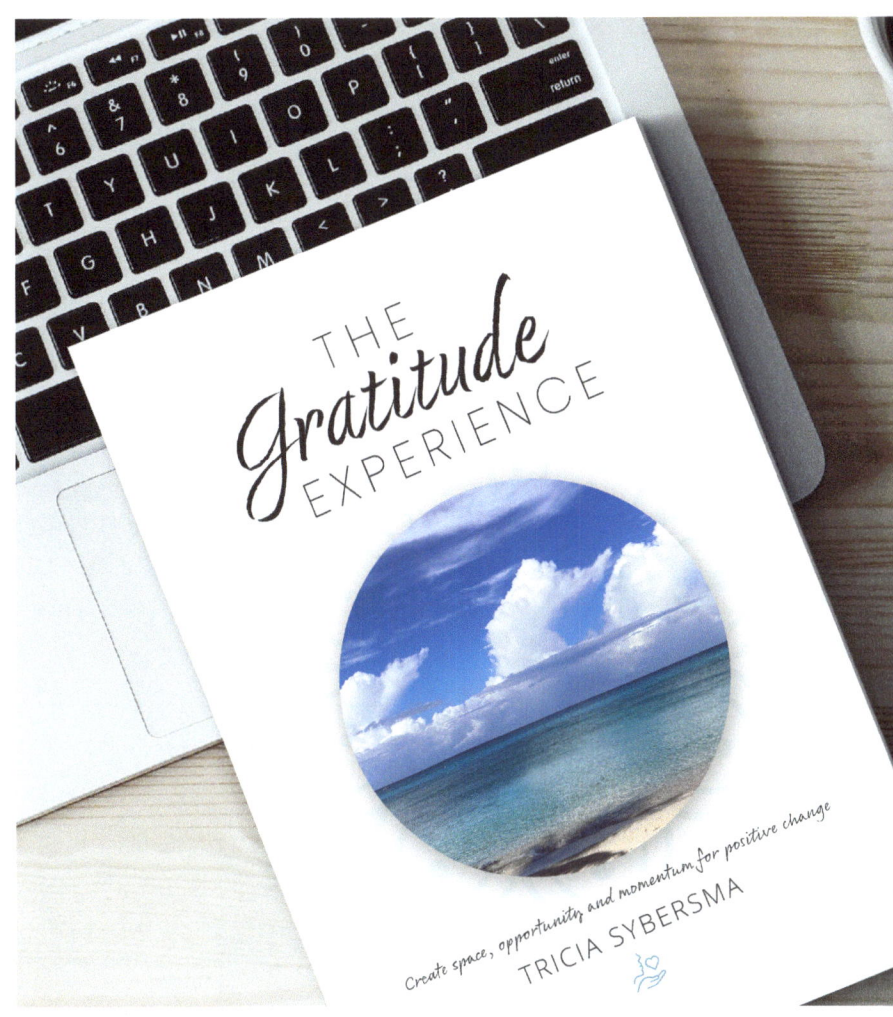

My Connection Story

Who else has felt like they don't fit in? Sharing childhood stories of being the last pick for teams at school are great icebreakers when meeting new people because on some level, everyone can relate. There is something very deep within us that seeks Connection.

Connection hub

When I was growing up, people were a mystery to me. I was awkward both socially and in sports, and therefore was last to be picked for teams, games, and clubs. I often felt like I didn't fit in. My strategy was to avoid interacting with people and instead seek Connections in nature and with animals, where I felt more comfortable. However, all this began to change in the most unlikely of places—the ultimate hub of global Connections. Airports!

Airports fascinate me. For many years I traveled through airports once a month, sometimes more. I remember my first few trips and how worried I was that I wouldn't know where to go or be able to find my next gate. Looking around, I was in awe of all the other travelers as they made their way around the airports. They made it look so easy and here I was, stressed, checking the monitors and hoping for the best.

Faking it

Then, something happened. I started to notice that I had misread the other travelers. Their fast-paced walking wasn't confidence but instead, it was them rushing to find their next gate because they were just as stressed and worried as I was. Suddenly, I went from feeling like I was the only one who had no idea what I was doing to realizing that no one does, we are all just faking it! This might sound odd, but I felt an immediate sense of relief and for the first time, I felt a sense of normalcy and belonging.

Field of Connection

This sparked my curiosity. I started to pay attention to people in general and realized that if I felt sad or happy, there was a good chance someone else was feeling sad or happy. If I felt like I didn't fit in, then for sure others felt like they didn't fit in. This led to the realization that how we feel, our experiences, and our stories are opportunities for powerful Connections.

This was just the beginning. I became fascinated with all the ways we are connected, how connections work and why they are so important to us. Connections are endless, and by sharing The Connection Experience, not only will you have the opportunity to explore and discover your own Connections, but also make many new ones.

WHAT IF YOU COULD CHANGE FROM FEELING LIKE YOU DON'T FIT IN, TO CELEBRATING HOW WE ARE ALL CONNECTED...

What is Connection?

This is one of those wonderful words that inspires questions and conversations. Therefore, a reliable source to turn to for clarity and understanding is a dictionary.

What does Connection mean?

The definition of connection is:

- The state of being connected
- The act of connecting two or more things
- Something that joins or connects two or more things
- A situation in which two or more things have the same connections (i.e., between thought and language)

*Source for all definitions within this book: www.merriam-webster.com

According to the definition, the word connection means many things, but what does it do? Using the definition, let's look at how Connections work by understanding what they do for us.

The term **state** is a good indicator of what connections do because it means readiness, stages of energy, and/or magnetic movement. Therefore...

> A Connection is dynamic. It has the ability to join two or more things and create an environment that attracts similar Connections and energies. "

What is the field of Connection?

The field of Connection is my way of describing existing and potential Connections available to us in every moment, both physical and energetic Connections. The word field is interesting. When I see the word field, my mind goes to images of wildflowers, hay, and horses. However, the word field means much more.

Definitions of field that may not be as familiar:

- For starters, the word field is a noun, verb, and adverb
- The sphere of practical operation outside a base, such as a laboratory
- Individuals that make up participants (i.e., in a contest)
- An area of an activity (i.e., the field of microbiology)
- A space in which a given effect exists (i.e., magnetic or gravitational)
- A complex of forces
- To take care of or respond to

The word "field" is the perfect word to encompass both our physical and energetic Connections.

What's in your field of Connection?

What comes to mind when you think about your field of Connection? Are any of these on your list? What would you add?

- Relationships
- Family and friends
- Places
- Careers
- Interests
- Sports
- Nature
- Pets
- Values
- Energy
- Yourself
- Add _____
- Add _____
- Add _____

What happened to our Connections?

We are born with strong Connections to ourselves and the people closest to us. Our survival depends on it. As we begin exploring as toddlers and young children, our Connections to nature and animals are natural. Just watch children play and get covered in dirt, and listen to their questions. They remind us just how magical the world truly is compared to how so many of us see it now.

> " Seek the wisdom of the ages but look at the world through the eyes of a child. "
> —Ron Wild

This quote highlights that no matter where we are on our journey, it is important to remember the natural curiosity and Connections we were born with.

Looking at what happened to our Connections helps us recognize and understand patterns.

Instead of going into judgement or criticism, let's observe from a place of gratitude. After all, this experience is about restoring our Connections to live life to its fullest.

Influences

In this context, influences are the "things" that can have an impact on our Connections. Something you may not have considered before is that influences themselves are neutral. It's how we respond to them that matters. Some influences can have a positive impact on our Connections, some can have a negative impact, and some have no impact at all. They include a wide range of situations, from a simple comment to a significant event.

Here is a short list of influences, with room to add your own:

- Family
- Peers
- Education
- Employment
- Social media
- Trends
- Marketing
- Entertainment
- World events
- Add _____
- Add _____
- Add _____

Recognizing when you are being influenced is an opportunity to increase your awareness. After all, an influence is a form of Connection, and you have the power to choose between being influenced or not, to engage with the Connection or set a boundary.

Getting in the Connection vibe

Before we move on, I invite you to take a few minutes and listen to "Connection" by One Republic.

Music is a wonderful way to experience Connection. The very nature of music is a multisensory field of Connections all on its own. Lyrics are an opportunity to connect to the story while our feet connect to the beat. Just try to sit still while listening!

Scan to Watch the Video

WHAT TO EXPECT DURING THE CONNECTION EXPERIENCE

You are about to begin a journey into the field of Connections to explore the two areas that influence how you participate in your life.

1. Connection to you

Here we will explore Connections to:

A. Your physical body
   - Bonus Section
B. Your energy
C. Your unique perspective
D. Your inner power
E. Boundaries

2. Connection to the world around you

Here we will discover your Connections to:

A. Nature
B. Community and beyond
C. Introduction to navigating

Throughout this experience, there are questions, activities, and music for you to enjoy and reflect on.

1. Connection to you

This is a celebration of you!

All of you, your physical body, your energy, your uniqueness, and your power.
In the busyness of everyday life, it's easy to forget how amazing you are.

Imagine what it would be like to have unlimited access to ALL of you.
Would you feel better, have more energy, more confidence, and a more powerful sense of YOU?

Are you ready to say YES? Because it all begins with your Connection to YOU.

Why me?

Who else is triggered when invited to do something for themselves? I have spent most of my life with thoughts that include, "I'm not good enough, not worthy, selfish," and more.

However, when you take a closer look, you will see why it is important to change from 'why me?' to **'why not me?'**.

As humans, we are designed to connect.

- We have physical bodies that see, smell, hear, taste, touch and are designed to connect with others and the world around us.

- We generate electromagnetic energy that is also designed to connect with others and the world around us.

Who remembers playing with magnets in science class? Watching them connect to other metal objects, surprised by the magnet's strength when removing objects from its magnetic force.

Guess what? You are that magnet connecting to any number of things in your field of Connections, with or without your participation in the process.

The Connection Experience starts with you because only you have the power to resist and decide your Connections.

Connections begin with me

Here are some of the benefits of connecting to you:

- Building a strong foundation
- Being present
- Feeling grounded
- A sense of calm
- Mind-body Connection
- Access to how your body feels and what it needs
- Access to your heart
- Access to your intuition
- Access to your hopes and dreams
- Discovering your unique perspective
- The ability to make decisions that are right for you
- The ability to set healthy boundaries
- Activating self-love
- Activating your inner power
- Add _____
- Add _____
- Add _____

What gets in the way?

- Too busy
- Self-criticism
- Lack of awareness
- Lack of confidence
- Lack of interest
- Lack of support
- Feeling ok
- Not feeling ok
- Pain
- Fatigue
- Add _____
- Add _____

> " The only thing you can be sure of is yourself. "

Now that you have explored the benefits and potential obstacles, let's begin to experience Connection to You, starting with your physical body.

> " *Sending Gratitude to your physical body leads to a better understanding of your Connection to the physical world and how Gratitude benefits both your relationship with yourself and nature.* "
>
> ~ The Gratitude Experience

A. Connection to your physical body

Your Connection starts here, with your physical body. Our physical body is how we show up; it is how we know we are alive, how we tell each other apart (unless you are identical twins). Can you image how confusing it would be if we all looked the same? There's a good reason why we have our own unique appearance.

It is through your physical body that you experience everything. We are all familiar with the five senses—sight, smell, sound, taste, and touch. It is through your physical body that you experience your first Connection while waiting to be born, through your early years, and throughout all the stages of your life.

Although there are aspects of your body that constantly change, both naturally and intentionally (like changing your hairstyle), the essence of your body doesn't change. Your one and only physical body is your companion throughout your entire life.

Suggestions to restore your Connection to your physical body

1 - BREATH

- Check in with your breath. Ask yourself, "How does breathing feel today?" Resist the temptation to change how you are breathing; instead, just notice.

- After a few breaths, or when you feel ready, go ahead and adjust your breathing to support how you are feeling. You may want to slow your breathing down, breathe a little deeper, or balance your inhale and exhale. If you're not sure, go ahead and explore. Your body will let you know what is the most supportive.

- Connecting to breath is a natural way to restore your Connection to your physical body and more. Breathing is the Connection between your physical body and energy. This explains why you can use breath to ground, center, and feel a sense of calm.

2 - BODY

- Try a body scan, or what I like to call MAT time: My Awareness Time. This can be done lying or sitting. Simply scan your body from head to toe to get a sense of how your body is feeling. A few minutes of MAT time on a regular basis will increase your awareness and Connection to your body. To get the most out of your MAT time, refer to The Gratitude Experience.

3 - SENSES

- Engage your five senses—sight, smell, sound, taste, and touch. You can go for a walk, take a bath, enjoy a meal, or snuggle under your favorite blanket and enjoy the sensations. You can mix it up; feel the warmth of the sun on your face and then imagine what that sounds like or tastes like. This is a fun way to really wake up your senses.

4 - HEART

- Connecting to your heart has many benefits, similar to connecting to your breath. In addition to the biological features, your heart has special neurons similar to those found in your brain. Connecting to these neurons is referred to as accessing your heart intelligence. When you connect to your breath, heart, and mind, you have access to a powerful Connection called coherence.

1 - Connection to you

HeartMath has techniques that restore and support your Connection to your heart, your heart intelligence, and brings your heart, mind, and energy into coherence. Take a few minutes and experience The Quick Coherence® Technique

> " *The HeartMath's definition of coherence is the state when the heart, mind and emotions are in energetic alignment and cooperation.* "
>
> ~ Dr. Rollin McCraty

BONUS SECTION
The Quick Coherence® Technique

 Step 1:
Focus your attention on the area of the heart. Imagine your breath is flowing in and out of your chest area, breathing a little slower and deeper than usual. Find an easy rhythm that's comfortable.

 Step 2:
As you continue heart-focused breathing, make a sincere attempt to experience a regenerative feeling, such as appreciation or care for someone or something in your life.

The Quick Coherence® technique was developed by and is a registered trademark of HeartMath.

You can use adjectives to describe your experience here:

_____

_____

*Mark this page so it is easy to find as you continue into
The Connection Experience*

B. Connection to your energy

Although you show up in a physical body, at a cellular level, you are also energy. Therefore, you are an amazing combination of both biological and energetic properties. Have you ever shocked yourself or someone else? Proof of your Connection to energy.

Your physical body depends on energy to function. It is your Connection to energy that keeps your heart beating, your lungs breathing, and your mind thinking. It is the spark of life itself.

Not only are we connected to and reliant on energy, but we also generate energy. In fact, we are amazing energy generators.

Did you know...

That while lounging on the couch, our physical body produces approximately 100 watts of power?
This is enough electrical energy to power a light bulb.

With effort (i.e., doing a cardio workout), we have the ability to generate over 2,000 watts of power!
Thank goodness we can just hit a switch to turn the lights on.

How do you feel?

This is a high-voltage question!
Who else has ignored, buried, or hidden their feelings?

Although our feelings are one of the most valuable parts of who we are, they are also one of our most vulnerable.

What does "how do you feel" mean?

There's a lot of confusion over the words feel, feelings, emotions, and even thought, yet they not only play a big part in our daily lives, they also generate lots of energy.

WHAT IS THE DIFFERENCE
between feelings, emotions, and thoughts?

The definition of feel is:
- Physical sensations
- Intuitive knowledge or ability

The definition of feeling is:
- An experience of an emotional state or reaction

The definition of emotion(s) is:
- A conscious mental reaction (such as joy or fear) experienced as strong feeling accompanied by physiological and behavioral changes in the body
- A state of feeling

The definition of thought is:
- An idea, plan, opinion, or picture that is formed in your mind
- The act or process of thinking

THE DIFFERENCE IS:
- **Feelings** are an intuitive experience of an emotion associated with our heart
- **Emotions** are a mental process associated with our mind
- **Thoughts** are a thinking process in our mind

For example, joy can be a feeling, an emotion, and a thought.
- When it is experienced in our heart, it is a feeling.
- When it is a mental process in our mind, it is an emotion.
- When it is an idea in our mind, it is a thought.

1 - Connection to you

Why is this important?

One word: Connection. Have you ever had to untangle the electrical cords under your computer desk? The process of figuring out which cord belongs to which device? Then the relief once it is all organized? The same is true for us. At any given moment, we are navigating a variety of feelings, emotions, and thoughts that are all creating energy. They can seem tangled, but you can start to untangle them.

01 Consider whether you are experiencing a feeling being generated in your heart, an emotion being processed in your mind, or a thought being formed in your mind?

02 Once you identify where the information is coming from, choose how you want to connect with it. For example, you can ask, "In this moment, is this information helpful or not?" If you decide it is helpful, then you can connect with it. If you decide it is not helpful at this time, you can either store it to use later, delete it, or change it.

> " *Not only can you untangle this energy, but you can also choose your Connection or change it!* "

Name that energy

Here is a fun way to develop your awareness and become comfortable with this group of energies.

- Throughout your day, challenge yourself to identify the energies you're experiencing and where they originate from.

- Is it a feeling in your heart, an emotion in your mind, a thought, or a combination? Resist the temptation to overthink, and just sense it. The best part is that you will always be right, because it is where you feel it.

The other way you can play this is to choose a feeling, such as hope.

- Activate the feeling of hope in your heart and notice.
  Next, activate the emotion of hope in your mind and notice.
  Then think about hope in your mind and notice.

What did you experience? Share what you noticed here:

_____

_____

Plugging into feelings

Between feelings, emotions, and thoughts, why focus on feelings? Because feelings are associated with heart energy, and connecting to your heart is the quickest way to restore Connection to all your energy.

Fun facts about feelings

They:
- Have a powerful influence on emotions, thoughts, and our physical body
- Provide a communication network between thoughts and emotions
- Are a conduit that connects heart and mind
- Generate frequencies and vibrational energies

In addition to choosing your thoughts and emotions, you also have the power to choose your feelings.

Vibes and feelings

Different feelings vibrate at different frequencies, ranging from lower vibrational frequencies, such as those associated with fear and anger, to higher vibrational frequencies associated with gratitude, care, and compassion. What's more, higher vibrational feelings like gratitude give us access to our heart energy and heart intelligence.

1 - Connection to you

THE DEFINITION OF HEART INTELLIGENCE:

> *The flow of awareness, understanding, and intuition we experience when the mind and emotions are brought into coherent alignment with the heart.*
>
> ~ HeartMath Institute

Choosing to activate and experience a high vibrational feeling opens the Connection that helps us shift into coherence.

Here is a list of high vibrational feelings. Select your favorites and/or add your own.

- Compassion
- Care
- Gratitude
- Joy
- Appreciation

- Kindness
- Add _____
- Add _____
- Add _____

Here are some of the benefits of being in coherence:

- Feeling more energized
- Being able to focus better
- Improved problem-solving

- Improved memory
- Increased intuition
- Increased creativity

This is all possible with The Quick Coherence® Technique.

There's no doubt that energy is a supercharged topic that affects our whole being. Focusing on feelings, emotions, and thoughts is an opportunity to gain a new appreciation for these energies and their impact on our daily life.

Restoring your Connection to these energies is the beginning of restoring your Connection to the wider network of energies.

What if you could restore your Connection to energy simply by caring?
The answer is, you can.

Care and Connection support each other.
When you care about something, you form a Connection, and when you form a Connection, you care.
~ Tricia Sybersma

Suggestions to restore your Connection to energy

1 - NOURISH

When we feel hungry, we nourish our body by getting something to eat. But what about our energy? Did you know that your energy needs nourishment too? Let's face it, we are busy, and often miss signs that our energy is getting low

These signs include:.

- Feeling tired
- Feeling irritable
- Feeling drained
- Lack of concentration
- Add _____
- Add _____

There is overlap between our physical body and energy, and it is important to take care of both. Simply recognizing when your energy is low jumpstarts the recharging process.

2 - NATURE

Nature is the natural charging station. Spending just a few minutes outside will recharge and nourish your energy. The fresh air, trees, plants, and even pots of seasonal flowers all help to calm and recharge both your energy and energy systems. Whether it is warm and sunny or cold and snowing, the weather also stimulates your senses to recharge your energy.

3 - LAUGHTER

A good joke, smiling, and finding something to giggle about will recharge and nourish your energy. Laughter releases endorphins, which decrease stress and promotes well-being. Laughter is also contagious; it not only benefits you, but also those around you.

4 - MUSIC

Listening to music, the frequencies and vibrations of your favorite songs, is a great way to recharge and nourish your energy. This is amplified even more when toe-tapping turns into dancing. Next time you need a quick pick-me-up, reach for your playlist, turn it up, and dance.

AS WE MOVE ONTO YOUR NEXT CONNECTION, ENJOY THE VIBE OF "CONNECTION" BY CAS HALEY

Scan to Watch the Video

C. Connection to your Unique Perspective (UP)

Someone once asked me, if I had a personal brand or product, what would it be? Without hesitation, my answer was Unique Perspective, or UP. From a young age, I saw things differently than my peers, coworkers, family, and friends—and was often criticized because of it.

- Who else can relate to the experience of seeing something differently?
- Feeling awkward and misunderstood?
- Do you see differently, or is it a question of perspective?

Our unique perspective is an accumulation of our experiences. Every person on the planet has a perspective based on their unique set of circumstances.

Restoring your Connection to your Unique Perspective is an opportunity to explore how you experience your life and the world around you; to see yourself as the amazing individual you are and to see others in a new way, encouraging and celebrating each other's unique talents and gifts.

What's up with your UP?

Viewing life experiences through your Unique Perspective is an invitation to shine a light into the deepest part of yourself and discover more of who you are.

However, for many of us, our Connection to our Unique Perspective has been compromised by the same influences that interfere with all our Connections (refer to list under Influences). Therefore, restoring Connection to our UP can be a profound and empowering experience.

It was only recently that I turned on my light and began to realize how important connecting to our Unique Perspective is, not only in understanding ourselves, but also in understanding others.

> *Your UP is how you experience your life. It's what makes you, YOU.*

Definitions

The meaning of the words unique and perspective may seem obvious, but there's often something interesting hiding in the definitions.

The definition of unique is:

- Being the only one
- Distinctively characteristic

The definition of perspective is:

- A mental view
- The interrelation in which a subject or its parts are mentally viewed; point of view
- The capacity to view things in their true relations or relative importance

The definition of point of view is:

- A position or perspective from which something is considered or evaluated

Therefore, in addition to being an accumulation of experiences, Unique Perspective is:

- A point of view or position that is relative to individual circumstances creating a filter through which you experience everything

What's so interesting about your UP?

Your unique perspective is smart technology that is constantly filtering information to protect and support you. It is continually updating and adjusting to new information and experiences to stay current. However, the most interesting aspect of your UP is the advanced settings that allow you to participate in the filtering process.

Why the focus on filtering?

We are surrounded by distractions that would overwhelm us physically and energetically if it weren't for a filtering system. This filtering system is based on previous experiences, information, and influences. It automatically filters your view of the world—with or without your participation.

Knowing this, wouldn't it be beneficial to be involved in the process? Here's how:
The definition of perspective includes the term point of view, which refers to a position. This means YOU have the power to change your position or view.

- You can change your position physically to get a better look at something
- You can also change your position energetically by choosing the feelings around an experience

When you choose the feeling(s), you change your point of view and perspective, which reprograms your filter. This not only works, but it is also backed by science and is part of HeartMath's Quick Coherence® Technique.

For instance, music. Who else disliked certain styles of music growing up? Then, at some point you experienced a change in your feelings. Maybe you noticed that certain styles of music lift your mood and help you feel better. Instead of avoiding those genres, you now have playlists.

The awareness that you have the power to change your perspective is life-changing, especially if the perspective you have isn't your own but is the result of influences. Once you discover how you really feel, you can change your UP to reflect the new you.

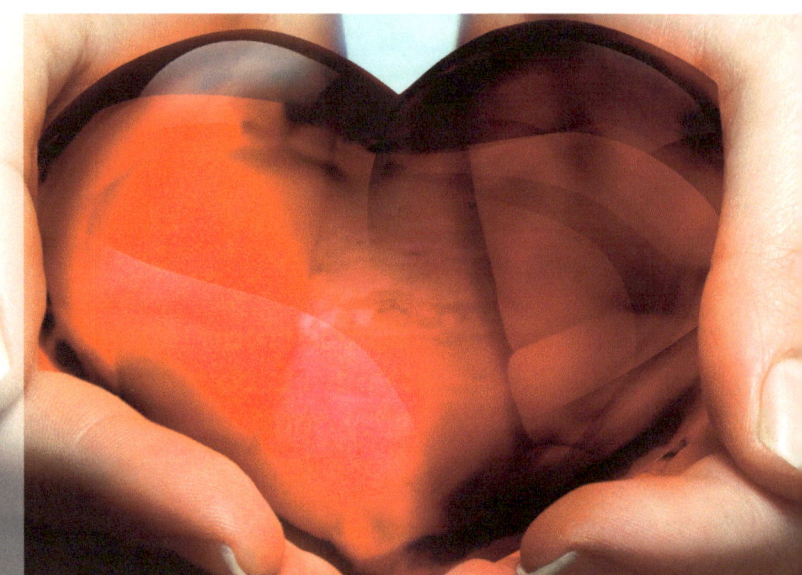

Where is your UP?

There are clues as to where your UP lives. For starters, your UP isn't physical, emotional, or a thought.

It is, however, related to feelings, and feelings are associated with the heart (refer to definition of feelings). **Therefore, your unique perspective lives in your heart.**

Experiences + Feelings = UP

Surprised? Here is some history. Our mind has been the focus of scientific study as the place where everything happens, but this is changing. New studies show what ancient practices like yoga have known for centuries—that our heart is actually the center of operations, and therefore home to your Unique Perspective. Hence the popular expressions referring to the heart space and heart center!

Minds are like a computer, busy storing and organizing all kinds of information. More often than not, our minds are quick to offer so much information that it creates confusion.

Our hearts, on the other hand, also have access to the information stored in our minds and more. Therefore, our heart has both physical and energetic properties that combine to form your Unique Perspective!

Working with your Unique Perspective

Start by discovering how you really feel about the world around you, your experiences, topics of interest, and the information you are exposed to.

Ask yourself this series of questions:

- How do I feel?
- Is how I'm feeling true?
- Is this how I want to feel?

If not, then choose how you want to feel. Use the Quick Coherence® Technique to activate the new feeling. Notice how the new feeling shifts your perspective. This shift in perspective will automatically update your filter. Invite your newly updated UP to help guide you and continue to update as needed.

For example, you find yourself in a situation that normally triggers anger and recognize that shifting to feelings of care and compassion would be beneficial. You can use the Quick Coherence® Technique to shift and change your feelings and perspective.

Can you list situations when this would be helpful?

_____

_____

Here are some of the ways UP supports you:

- Helps you discover how you really feel
- Creates awareness of what is important to you
- Increases access to your creativity and intuition
- Acts as an inner guidance system
- Filters influences and information
- Builds confidence and the ability to trust yourself
- Helps when making decisions
- Add _____
- Add _____
- Add _____

Did you know...

The average person makes 35,000 choices each day, 2,000 decisions per hour, or 1 decision every two seconds.

~ Psychology Today

When we connect to and start working with our UP, not only do we shine a light into who we are, but we also see others as unique individuals.

This generates understanding, compassion, and creates wonderful opportunities to share knowledge and information, and learn from each other.

UP and your unique expression

As you develop your relationship with your Unique Perspective, something else begins to emerge—your unique expression. This is because your UP is an access point into your intuition and imagination. Intuition is also referred to as the sixth sense, and maybe imagination is the seventh. You are the only one who can access your intuition and imagination, explore your inner world, and bring forth insight, creativity, and your unique expression.

> *The things that make me different are the things that make me.*
> ~ Winnie the Pooh

Imagination and intuition

The definition of intuition is:

- The power or faculty of attaining direct knowledge or cognition without evident rational thought and inference
- Quick and ready insight

The definition of imagination is:

- The act or power of forming a mental image of something not present to the senses or never before wholly perceived in reality
- Creative ability

The difference is:

Intuition accesses information, and imagination accesses something new. Not only do they complement each other, they offer balance.

We've all heard the expression, "It's just your imagination running away with you." Your intuition provides balance for imagination, and imagination provides creativity for our intuition. You have access to both of these powerful resources through your UP. (It's interesting that both definitions start with the word power.)

Connecting to your intuition and imagination is a wonderful way to invite your UP and UE to show up and activate.

> **" Your Unique Expression is your Unique Perspective in action! "**

Unique activities to restore your Connection to your UP

1 - CREATE

Discover what creative activities make your heart sing. Being creative is a wonderful way to connect to your feelings. When you connect to your feelings, you connect to your UP.

Start now by noticing the feelings that are activated as you look at this list.

- Gardening
- Painting
- Writing
- Music
- Dancing
- Designing
- Cooking
- Add _____
- Add _____
- Add _____

2 – SENSE

Our senses are constantly sending us valuable feedback and information. Being aware of the feedback from your senses is another lens into our UP, like sight, for instance.

List your three **favourite** colors:

- _____
- _____
- _____

- What do you like about these colors?
- Are you drawn to them because they are trendy on social media and fashion, or do you really like them?

How do these colours make you feel? _____
_____

List three colors you **don't like**:

- _____
- _____
- _____

- What don't you like about these colors?
- Are you repelled by them because they are overused in some way, or do you really not like them?

How do these colours make you feel? _____
_____

- Compare your experience between the colors you like and don't like.
- Describe the difference in a way that makes sense to you.

_____
_____
_____

You can apply this practice to other themes, like food and entertainment, by inviting your senses to participate in the filtering process. You may even discover that you like some things you thought you didn't, and vice versa.

1 - Connection to you

3 - NOTICE

Become aware of external influences, including:

- Opinions
- Social-media
- Entertainment
- Add _____
- Add _____
- Add _____

By simply noticing when and how you're being influenced, those influences will start to lose their power, and will no longer be effective.

> " *Your UP is a light radiating from your heart space. Use this light to illuminate how you see the world around you and to focus on what's important.* "

4 - EXPLORE

As you go about your day, be open to opportunities to explore how you really feel about everyday things, such as places, activities, and even conversations. Have a sense of adventure, curiosity, and most importantly, humor, as you discover your true feelings.

D. Connection to your Inner Power

CONNECTING TO YOUR INNER POWER IS ACTION

You have restored Connections to your physical body, energy, and Unique Perspective. What's next? It's time to say hello to your Inner Power.

What does Inner Power mean to you?

- ◯ Motivation
- ◯ Confidence
- ◯ Contentment
- ◯ Independence
- ◯ Energy
- ◯ Creativity
- ◯ Add _____
- ◯ Add _____

Yes, it is all this and more. When you restore Connections to your body, energy, and UP, there is an alignment, an invitation into something deeper and expansive at the same time, the access point to a portal of a self-sustaining energy source powering you from within. **This is your Inner Power.**

The definition of power is:

- ◯ The ability to act or produce an effect
- ◯ Mental or moral efficacy (the power to produce an effect)
- ◯ A source or means of emitting and supplying energy, especially electricity

Therefore, Inner Power is:

- ◯ The **ability** and **power** to create.
- ◯ The **alignment** of life force energy + mental energy + heart energy = Inner Power

Where is Inner Power?

Inner Power radiates from our heart, or heart space. Although the ability to create is associated with mental energy in our mind, the power to create is associated with the heart. Therefore, the heart space is where ability and power meet and merge.

Since feelings are also associated with the heart space, choosing a high-vibrational feeling, such as gratitude, gives us access to even more heart energy to work with.

Did you know...

That our heart is 100 times stronger electrically and 5,000 times stronger magnetically than our brain? "The human heart has recently come to be documented and studied as the strongest organ in the human body regarding generation of electric and magnetic fields.
~ HeartMath

What's the connection between our UP and Inner Power?

Unique Perspective is associated with heart energy. Inner Power introduces mental energy associated with our mind. They are the perfect complement to each other. Mental energy offers ideas and information that is filtered through your UP. The ideas that pass through your filters are then fueled with heart energy into existence by creating and manifesting.

What fuels your Inner Power?

Heart energy is what fuels our Inner Power. Our heart is fueled by a combination of energy generated by biology, function, and the energy of our feelings.

What fuels our feelings?

Our feelings are fueled by the energy generated by how we experience the world around us through our Unique Perspective.

 It is your ability to choose your thoughts and feelings that ultimately fuels your Inner Power.

What is the connection between Inner Power and ego?

Who else has blamed their ego for their choices and actions?
Ego is one of the most studied and written about themes, yet it remains a mystery. Let's unravel ego by going back to the basics.

Definition of ego:
- The self, especially as contrasted with another self or the world (opposite of the definition of connection)

Definition of self:
- An individual's typical character or behavior
- An individual's temporary behaviour

History
- The Latin root word for ego means "I"

Based on these definitions, ego is associated with mental energy and separation, which is opposite of Connection. Therefore, more Connection = less ego.

Instead of more explanations of what ego is, let's send care and understanding towards our ego and take positive action with an affirmation like this:
I connect to my Inner Power and choose my behavior in all things. So it is.

Benefits of connecting to your Inner Power:

- Gain access to your field of connections
- Gives you the ability to manifest and create
- Powers your UP
- Enhances your GPS
- Helps you set boundaries
- Add _____
- Add _____

"I connect to my Inner Power and choose my behavior in all things.
SO, IT IS."

Suggestions to restore Connection to your Inner Power

1 - EXPAND

Learning is a great way to connect and expand your Inner Power. Do you have topics of interest you've been putting off? Now is the time. Learning about astrology, astronomy, crystals, and healing modalities will not only expand your Inner Power but may even turn out to be a passion and financial opportunity.

List your interests here:

- _____
- _____
- _____

- _____
- _____
- _____

2 - MEDITATE

Before assuming meditation is a complicated, boring, or difficult activity, let's look at the definition:

- To engage in contemplation or reflection
- To engage in mental exercise such as concentration on one's breathing for the purpose of reaching a heightened level of spiritual awareness
- To focus one's thoughts
- To plan or project in the mind

What if meditating is simply checking your connections? When you check in with your physical body, energy, UP, and Inner Power, you are engaging with the definition and therefore meditating!

3 - MANIFEST

One of the benefits of connecting to your Inner Power is creating and manifesting. Easier said than done...or is it?

What is manifesting?

The definition of manifest is:

- Easily understood or recognized by the mind, obvious
- Readily perceived by the senses, especially by the sense of sight

Therefore, to manifest means to create something that is easily recognizable, like a chair. No wonder the topic of manifesting is the subject of mixed reviews. It is easy to see why when you compare the definition to the hype that manifestation is surrounded in mystery and magic.

At first glance, there is no reference to anything magically appearing in the definition… or is there?

The reference to senses is a clue. Senses are associated with feelings, which are associated with heart energy.

Therefore, there is a magical power in manifesting when approached in a practical yet heart-centered way.

THE NEXT PAGE INTRODUCES YOU TO AN EASY WAY TO START MANIFESTING.

 *1 - Connection to you*

ONE MINUTE *Manifest*

6. How will this change my life!

1. What do I want?

5. How can I make this bigger?

2. How will I feel when it arrives?

4. Why do I want it?

3. What support do I need?

Scan to print

1 - Connection to you

How to work with the One-Minute Manifest

The Center – represents your heart energy.
- Add something personal: a word, picture, or simply a smiley face

1. What do you want?
- Make it obvious
- This can be something physical, like a car or energy, like practicing more gratitude
- Include lots of details, then add some more

2. How will you feel when it arrives?
- Spend time experiencing how you will feel after successfully manifesting
- This activates your heart energy (the magic)
- Invite and allow your heart energy and the universe to do the rest

3. What support do you need?
- Don't be shy, include everything you need

4. Why do you want this?
- Is it for practical reasons?
- Is it your hopes and dreams?
- Maybe a combination

5. How can you make this bigger?
- Be careful not to limit the outcome; leave room for growth

6. How will this change your life?
- This is the perfect opportunity to add the energy of gratitude to your One-Minute Manifest

When you're satisfied with your effort
- Add the date
- Put your One-Minute Manifest somewhere you will remember
- Feel free to add more details at any time
- After a week, month, or year, take a look and be amazed
- You can make as many One-Minute Manifests as you like. **Enjoy!**

Manifesting works from the inside out, starting with the
MAGICAL POWER OF HEART ENERGY = FEELINGS

E - Boundaries

As interesting as expanding, meditating, and manifesting are in restoring your Connection to your Inner Power, Connections themselves can be overwhelming. Therefore, it is never too early to start setting boundaries. Your Inner Power gives you everything you need to choose between what you want to connect to and what you don't.

Favorite song

- Who else has listened to a song and knew right away if you liked it or not?
- How do you know this?
- Is it how the song made you feel, the lyrics, easy to dance to?

The same applies to Connections.

Super quick guide for setting boundaries

- If it's a song or Connection you like, engage, give it attention and energy, add it to your playlist
- If it isn't, don't engage or give it energy by simply skipping to the next one
- If it's something that's been on your playlist for a while and it no longer resonates, you can set a boundary by disengaging and clicking delete.

Developing good boundaries now will help you as you start exploring the greater Field of Connections. You are invited to a deeper dive into boundaries in **Community and Beyond.**

ENJOY "CONNECTION" BY THE GREEN CHILDREN AS WE BEGIN EXPERIENCE #2.
CONNECTION TO THE WORLD AROUND YOU.

Scan to Watch the Video

2. Connection to the world around you

This is an invitation to bring what you've learned into the world around you and beyond.

Experiencing the world from the lens of Connection opens up exciting new ways to explore our Connections with nature and our communities, as well as expanding beyond our communities to discover how we are connected to all humanity, the planet, and the universe.

Learn how to work with your Field of Connections and choose the Connections that are right for you.

Why is this important?

Good question. The simple answer is—to provide you with information and tools to help you navigate your life from a place of understanding and purpose while making decisions and creating opportunities to not only live your life, but also to love your life.

> *Experience for yourself how all roads lead home as you continue to strengthen your Connections.*

Here are some of the benefits of connecting to the world around you:

- Spend more time outside
- Health and wellness
- A sense of curiosity
- A sense of balance
- A sense of harmony
- Compassion towards yourself
- Compassion towards others
- Confidence
- The ability to look within
- The ability to protect your energy
- Trust in yourself
- Sense of purpose
- Increased focus
- Navigating with confidence
- Add _____
- Add _____

What gets in the way?

- ⚪ Lack of time
- ⚪ Lack of interest
- ⚪ Feeling overwhelmed
- ⚪ Feeling insignificant
- ⚪ Lack of boundaries
- ⚪ Lack of reward
- ⚪ Lack of energy
- ⚪ Add _____
- ⚪ Add _____
- ⚪ Add _____

I invite you to turn these obstacles into opportunities as you begin the journey of connecting to the world around you.

> *"When we understand how Connection's work, we can choose to participate in the process for powerful results."*

A. Connection to nature

Nature surrounds us; it is us on so many levels. Even saying the word is soothing somehow. Let's begin with the obvious. We live in a physical body in a physical world, but what's not so obvious is how amazing this really is. Sadly, in our so-called modern societies, many of us have schedules and commitments that challenge daily interactions with nature.

What does nature mean to you?

_____

What is nature?

In gematria (the numeric value of words), the value for nature is shared with the words mother, alpha omega, flower, loving, laughter, listen, and be still. The dictionary adds more interesting clues.

The definition of nature is:

- The physical world and everything in it, such as plants, animals, mountains, oceans, stars, everything that is not made by people
- A creative and controlling force in the universe
- The natural forces that control what happens in the world such as weather and gravity
- An inner force such as instinct, appetite or desire
- The way that a person or animal behaves, their character or personality

Nature is a combination of natural, inner, and creative forces similar to us.

- Natural forces in nature include the vast variety of physical world
- Natural forces we share include what we experience with our senses
- Inner forces in nature include energies generated by wind, water, and weather
- Inner forces we share include energies generated by our thoughts, emotions, and feelings
- Creative forces in nature include the shaping of the land, resources, and food
- Creative forces we share include our ability to reproduce, make things, and solve problems

This reflects the relationship between the natural realm and the human realm, highlighting that we have more in common than we realize.

We also share:

- Biology; minerals, proteins, cellular structure, geometry
- Four elements—water, fire, air, earth
- Cycles, seasons, life and death

Most importantly, we share layers of symbiotic relationships.

Above all else, Earth is home, where we live. There is a saying, "The Earth doesn't need us, but we need the Earth." This is true. We can move to a different town, city or country but we can't move to a different planet.

We rely on nature's ability to maintain an atmosphere and environment that makes it possible for us to exist and thrive. By restoring our Connection with nature, we develop an even deeper Connection to our ourselves.

2 - Connection to the world around you

 Restoring our Connection to nature is an invitation to connect to something bigger, something we need, rely on, and take care of. Something that connects us all. That something is our home.
~ Tricia Sybersma

 ## Activities to restore your Connection to nature

1 - NOTICE

Who else can go a whole day without noticing if it's sunny or cloudy outside? It takes effort to notice. It's good to know that the effort is rewarded with the benefits associated with being in nature. It only takes a few minutes to improve overall feelings of wellness.

Next time you are outside, notice what catches your eye.

- A tree rustling its leaves as if to wave hello
- The way the sun shines on a flower
- The shape of the clouds
- A bird chirping
- Add _____
- Add _____

As you begin to notice nature, just maybe, nature begins to notice you. Remember, the value for the word nature is the same as mother, alpha omega, flower, loving, laughter, listen, and be still. These words not only describe nature, but also how to restore our Connection to the natural world around us.

2 - CARE

It's a fact; when we care about something, we take better care. A fresh way to look at the word CARE is: Curious Action Responsible for the Environment.
Here are some ideas to turn this acronym into taking care:

A fresh way to look at CARE

CURIOUS – Learn something new specific to your area.

ACTION – Commit to one small step in support of what you learned.

RESPONSIBLE – Identify ways you can promote awareness for yourself and others.

ENVIRONMENT – Realize that caring for the environment is simply an extension of self-care.

Share your plan to CARE.
_____

3 - HEAL

In addition to improving overall feelings of wellness, being in nature heals by improving:

- Mood
- Energy
- Immune system
- Creativity
- Add _____
- Add _____

There's more. Our bodies are designed to benefit from direct contact with the earth. When we walk barefoot or place our bare hands on the earth, we absorb negative ions, which reduce inflammation and restore balance to our bodily systems. No wonder spending time gardening or taking a long walk on the beach has such a profound effect. Nature is helping you reboot your whole body with a simple touch.

4 - PLAY

Spending time outside hiking, at the beach, or in the snow encourages play, and for good reason. Not only does play and laughter promote good health for us, the sound of having fun is a welcome vibration that benefits nature.

Studies have shown that speaking kindly to plants helps them grow faster.

The next time you are outside, play, laugh, and really enjoy yourself. Go ahead and jump in the pile of fall leaves or dance in the rain. Have fun building a sandcastle or a snowman. Not only will you be smiling, but nature will also be smiling back at you.

B. Connection to community and beyond

Throughout the Connection Experience, something amazing has been emerging. That something is YOU. An understanding of not only who you are, but also how powerful and magical you are.

Choose four adjectives to describe what you have discovered about yourself:

- _____
- _____
- _____
- _____

Discovering more about yourself is another opportunity for self-care and is empowering. This leads to the next questiont: what to do with the new you? In this section, we will look at restoring Connection to community while honoring yourself.

What is community?

The definition of community is:

- A group of people who live in the same area, such as a city, town or neighbourhood
- A group of people who have the same interests
- A group of nations

Therefore, community is when we are with others.

2 – Connection to the world around you

People gather in communities for lots of reasons, including:

- Shared interests
- Companionship
- Work
- Support
- Resources
- Protection
- Add _____
- Add _____

There is another important reason for community, and that is Connection. A huge turning point for me was recognizing that it isn't 'fitting in' we seek, but the feeling of Connection.

Let's compare the difference between fitting in and Connection.

Fitting in

- The same
- Accept
- Agree
- Compliant
- Uniform

Connection

- Appreciated
- Valued
- Heard
- Included
- Respected for your differences
- Encouraged to participate
- Add _____
- Add _____

Fitting in is associated with the mind and ego; Connection is associated with feelings and heart energy. When there is Connection, there is an absence of ego, competitiveness, jealousy, and other energies that can cause unhealthy division, whereas Connection promotes togetherness through understanding and cooperation.

The good news is that in your field of community Connections, you have permission to choose between fitting in or making heartfelt Connections.

Boundaries

Once you understand that you are designed to connect, participate, and choose your Connections, setting boundaries is the next step.

How do you know when to set a boundary? By how you feel. Whether this is a new Connection or a Connection with years of history, there may come a time when that Connection is no longer serving you and it is time to set a boundary.

If you experience one or more of the items below, you may need to set boundaries:

- Fatigue
- Tension
- Irritation
- Restless
- Restricted
- Prickly
- Add _____
- Add _____

Fun fact

Do you know that our gut is a reflection of our heart? If our heart is sensing that something is out of balance (not good for us), it sends a message to our gut to alarm us to pay attention; that something's not right. This warning system works so well that it is often referred to as "gut instinct." It's a relief to know that our heart and gut are working together and looking out for our highest good.

The benefits of setting boundaries include:

- Protects your energy
- Protects your relationships
- Sends clear intentions of what you want to attract
- Helps manage expectations
- Helps align your hopes and dreams

Setting boundaries

The easiest way to set a boundary is simply by not engaging. If an opportunity comes up and you decide it's not for you right now, be honest with yourself and the people involved. Use your energy and disengage. This is a clean and polite way of saying no, and you will thank yourself later.

How to disengage

You can disengage your energy by shifting into neutral. Practice being neutral so you are comfortable going there when that's the best place to be.

2 - Connection to the world around you

Practice makes perfect

To practice being neutral, start with something familiar, like going to your favorite place for lunch. Allow yourself to feel the excitement, then shift into neutral and feel the difference.

PRACTICE SHIFTING FROM FEELING EXCITED TO NEUTRAL AND BACK TO EXCITED.
This is training for your emotions and feelings.

Once you are comfortable shifting in familiar experiences, try other types of experiences so no matter what, you are able to shift into neutral.

Coherence and community

Do you know that connecting to your heart and shifting into coherence not only has personal benefits, but also has benefits that expand into our Connections and communities?

'Connections to You' introduced The Quick Coherence® Technique.

You learned how shifting into coherence helps restore Connections to our physical heart, feelings, heart energy, and heart intelligence.

There's more—when you shift into coherence, not only are there changes inside your body, but also changes to the energy you radiate into the space around you.

> *When in coherence, you are radiating heart energy out into your communities, which can be referred to as "Feeding the Field"*
> ~ Dr. Rollin McCraty

Bonus info ~ Your heart produces an electromagnetic field surrounding your body 360 degrees, extending beyond the skin out into space, measurable up to about three feet outside your body.

"Information about a person's emotional state is encoded in the heart's magnetic field and is communicated throughout the body and into the external environment."

~ HeartMath®

2 – Connection to the world around you

**ENJOY THIS LOVELY SONG ABOUT COMMUNITY
"CONNECTION" BY DEVA PREMAL AND MITEN**

Beyond

Welcome to the beyond! We've all heard the phrase "We are all connected" and wondered if this is true. Instead of focusing on what we don't know, let's explore what we do know.

We know:
- Our composition is the same as the earth's
- The composition of the earth is the same as star dust and the universe
- Information and energy are shared between us and the natural world
- Information and energy are shared between us and the universe through astrology and astronomy

The definition of astrology is:
- The intuitive perception of the stars and planets on human affairs and terrestrial events by their positions and aspects

The definition of astronomy is:
- The study of objects and matter outside the earth's atmosphere and of their physical and chemical properties

What's the difference?

Astrology refers to the **energetic** properties and Astronomy refers to the **physical** properties of the stars, planets and their movement.
BOTH ENERGETIC AND PHYSICAL PROPERTIES HAVE A PROFOUND EFFECT ON US HERE ON EARTH

2 - Connection to the world around you

Curiosities

- Do our actions, thoughts, and feelings ripple around the Earth?
- How far do our connections expand into the beyond?
- Are we, in fact, all connected?

These curiosities are an invitation for personal reflection.

- It is important to get a sense of how you see yourself in the big picture.
- It is valuable in the sense of belonging, purpose, and most importantly, to know and understand that you and everything you do matters.

 When I reflect on these questions, I look to the teachers who have been with us from the beginning; **THE NATURAL WORLD AND THE UNIVERSE.**

It is easy to forget that we are an active part of the universe; that the universe is not some faraway place we only see in the movies, but is an extension of our home, and that each one of us is a unique expression of the universe.

Patterns

When questions and concepts are big, one way to gain clarity and find common ground is by looking for patterns. Let's see what our relationship with the universe looks like using patterns.

The moon orbits the Earth. The Earth, with the other planets in our solar system, orbits the sun. Our sun and solar system are part of The Milky Way galaxy which orbits The Great Central Sun, and maybe The Great Central Sun orbits an even bigger sun.

The pattern is that although the Earth is part of larger systems, it maintains its own identity and orbit, despite everything else going on around it. Yes, there may be astrological and astronomical influences like solar flares and asteroids, but the Earth stays on course within varying degrees.

How does this relate to us?

You are living your life closely surrounded by your core group of family and friends (your moons). You are also part of larger systems and groups, which include your communites, where you live, work, and play. This expands to include even larger systems, such as countries, corporations, travel, family and friends in different parts of the world. These systems continue to expand and eventually include all humans and the entire planet.

The pattern is that, despite all these systems and distractions, you maintain your own identity, goals, hopes, dreams, and your own unique orbit . There will be influences, obstacles, challenges, and opportunities along the way, but you have the power to stay true to yourself and on course (allowing for some wiggle room).

There are so many wonderful ways to explore what nature and the universe have to teach us that this is the theme of my next series of books called **Live Like a Planet.** Where you are invited to join me in a fun, new way to look at understanding life as Planet You. COMING SOON.

Did you know...

Six degrees of separation is the idea that all people are six or fewer social connections away from each other.

 ## Suggestions to restore your Connection to communities and beyond

1 - SAY YES

A wonderful way to restore your Connection to your community is to choose where to invest your energy. Find out what's aligned with your interests, goals, hopes, and dreams, and say yes to connecting. See how many ways you can expand your network in areas that interest you.

List your interests here.

- _____
- _____

2 - SAY NO

Saying no sounds easier said than done. However, setting boundaries is caring for both yourself and the other person and/or group. Start by saying no to small requests. Remember that it is helpful to disengage your energy by simply shifting into neutral. If you're not sure if the opportunity is right for you, check in with your gut. As your confidence grows, you will refine your no. Soon, setting boundaries will become second nature.

3 - DISCOVER

Apply what you've learned about boundaries to learn something new. As you consider topics, check in with your heart and your gut to discern if this topic is worth your time, effort, and energy. You might find that your interests change and topics that weren't of interest suddenly are.

4 - REFLECT

Bigger questions and concepts require some time and space. Notice and allow time to reflect or meditate. Both are effective; however, there is a difference.

- Reflecting is thinking deeply. It is active, and can be done anywhere, anytime, like standing in line at the grocery store.
- Meditation, on the other hand, is about focus, stillness, and silence.

Therefore, to reflect is meditation on the go!

Try both and see which one suits you. Have a journal handy so you can make note of insights.

2 - Connection to the world around you

C. Introduction to navigating

Let's begin with a question.

If you were to pick one word to summarize why you are here on this planet, what would that word be?

_____

My word is 'navigating'!

Everything we do involves some element of navigating. Even choosing to love involves the choice to love, which includes navigating that choice. Now that you have restored your Connections to you, your communities, and beyond, participating in how you move through your life becomes important and meaningful.

Definition of navigate:
- To find the way to get to a place
- To travel on, over, or through
- To steer a course

Things we navigate
- Daily routines
- Schedules
- Grocery stores
- Thoughts
- Problems
- Expectations
- Relationships
- Trips
- Short- and long-term goals
- Careers
- Add _____
- Add _____

The layers we navigate:
- Physically, as we move our physical bodies in this physical world
- Energetically with our thoughts, feelings, and relationship with energy
- Directionally, as we move towards, around, and away from something and decision-making

The tools:
- Understanding how Connections work
- Being aware of challenges (i.e., influences)
- How to use The Quick Coherence® Technique
- The power of choosing your feelings
- Connecting to your UP
- Connecting to your inner power
- Setting boundaries
- Being true to yourself and staying on course
- Honoring your unique presence in the world and universe

The power source
- Both your heart and mind generate an unlimited supply of electromagnetic energy
- The properties include electric and magnetic, forces that attract, repel, and deflect

Therefore, navigating is:
- A combination of movement and attraction
- It is two friends running towards each other, both moving and attracting until they connect in a welcoming embrace
- It is also the power to deflect and repel unwanted interaction
- Most importantly, it is the ability to sit in the driver's seat of your life

Compass

Did you know that not only do you have an inner compass, but it has been your GPS throughout your life? Your inner compass is directly influenced by the alignment of your thoughts and feelings. When thoughts and feelings don't align, our compass struggles to find a clear way forward.

Mapping
Imagine your life as a map.
- Where do your thoughts land on the map?
- Where do your feelings land on the map?
- Do they align with where you want to go?

2 - Connection to the world around you

> When we truly know
> where we are,
> we are *ready to see*
> *where we are going.*
> ~ *Tricia Sybersma*

Destinations

Where do you see yourself:

- Today
- This week
- A year from now?

Working with destinations helps us to know where we are and identify where we want to go. Focusing on your destination is a wonderful complement to manifesting.

The definition of destination:

- The purpose for which something is predetermined or destined
- An act of appointing, setting aside for a purpose
- A place to which one is journeying

Therefore, a destination is a combination of purpose and location. Knowing where you are going and why you want to go there.

What is the difference between manifesting and destination?

- Manifesting is **activating** heart energy to attract and/or create with your thoughts
- Destination is **aligning** heart energy and thoughts to go somewhere and/or do something

In addition to being a physical location, a destination may also include a change of attitude, such as being more patient and understanding. Both manifesting and destination have a relationship with physical and energetic properties.

How to set a destination:
There's two key parts to setting a destination

- Know where you want to go
- Know why you want to go there

These two keys will help align your thoughts and feelings and provide a clear way forward for your inner compass.

You can manifest a destination
or let a destination inspire what to manifest.

True Story

Navigating my way from one gate to another in the Miami airport, I was having a deep discussion with myself over the quote, "You are not your thoughts," by Eckhart Tolle. If I'm not my thoughts, then who am I?

In that moment, I realized that I am my focus. This gave me lots to ponder during my next flight. It makes perfect sense because what we focus on, we become. Choosing your focus helps shift everything into alignment and you're ready to set off to your destination.

The superpower of setting a destination is FOCUS.

 Planning your next destination?
USE THIS CHECKLIST TO JUMPSTART YOUR CONNECTION TO NAVIGATING.

1. Where do you want to go? Is it a place, a change of attitude, or a combination of both?
_____

2. What does this involve? List as many details as possible
_____

3. Am I ready to do the work? _____

4. Am I ready to say yes to the outcome? _____

5. How do I want to feel when I arrive at my destination?
_____

6. Now relax and enjoy the journey. This is the secret to successful navigating.

Time to Fuel-up

Fuel-up with the energy of gratitude to super charge your focus
Use **The Quick Coherence Technique** (pg. 15) to activate your heart energy

The benefits of enjoying the journey include:

- A better overall view
- Attracting more options
- Ability to shift and make decisions that serve you

This checklist will also help you identify areas that require homework for the best possible outcome.
Sometimes when we plan for one thing and something completely different shows up, it can be an imbalance in alignment. When we exceed expectations, it reflects optimal alignment. Once satisfied with the checklist, you are ready to navigate.

Wrapping up with affirmations

Congrats! You have arrived. You understand Connections and have the power to choose the Connections that are right for you and navigate to your destination.

BEFORE YOU GO, A GIFT.

Affirmations

There's an easy way to create personal affirmations to support you on your journey.

Definition of affirmation

- To affirm, show or express a strong belief in or dedication to something such as a good idea
- Affirmations are a powerful source of support, encouragement, and commitment as you continue your Connection experience.

Create your affirmation

Here are some key words that will continue to support you and your journey:

> *breath, body, senses, heart, nourish, nature, laughter, music, create, sense, notice, explore, expand, meditate, manifest, boundaries, notice, care, heal, play, say yes, say no, discover, reflect*

I invite you to use these words and complete the affirmation statements below. Let these words inspire, support, and encourage you. Please feel free to add to this list.

Example

- **I will** nourish my heart with laughter.
- **I promise** to notice nature, explore, reflect, and breathe.
- **I am** saying yes to manifesting.
- **I am grateful** for my body and boundaries.

 **Your affirmation**

- **I will** _____
- **I promise** _____
- **I am** _____
- **Add your own** _____
  ie, I am grateful

Use this to create personal affirmations as often as you like. Write them out and remember to put them where you will see them.

A GIFT FOR YOU!
For more fun, take a look at the "Be Your Own Cheerleader" e-mini and create even more affirmations - my gift to you!

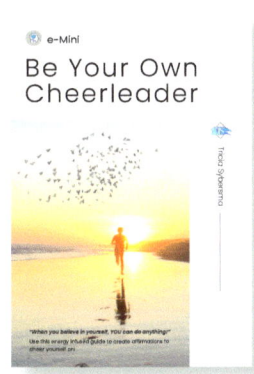

SCAN the QR code below to download your free gift now.

The password is 'connection'

AND NOW IT'S TIME TO JUST DANCE WITH "CONNECTION" BY YCTAEYANG

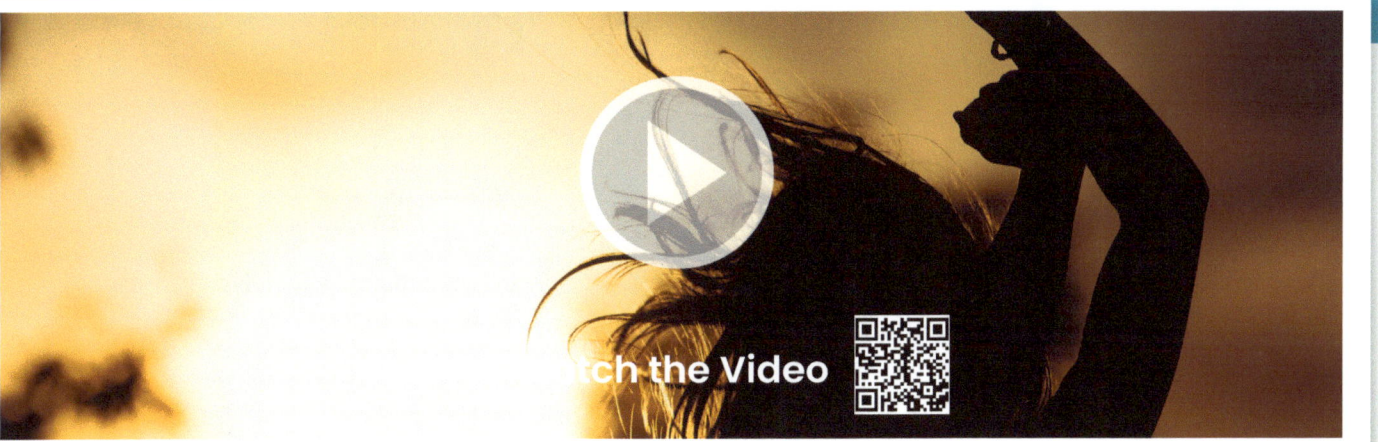

Thank you!

For being part of this journey with me.
I look forward to our next adventure.

Tricia Sybersma

The Connection Collection

*Experience Connections **to self**, community and beyond*

The Connection Collection is a powerful set of programs designed to help you dive deep into the energy of connection for greater self-awareness and personal growth.

This collection provides a wealth of resources to help you stay focused and motivated on your journey toward greater connection and consciousness. Whether you're looking to break free from old patterns or cultivate a deeper sense of connection in your daily life, this collection has something for you.

The Connection Experience
You are invited to explore the power of connection for self-awareness and personal growth. Whether you're looking to improve your relationships, manifest your goals, or simply connect more deeply with your inner wisdom, *The Connection Experience* can help you tap into the power of connection and use it to create positive change in your life.

Your Connection Experience Notebook
A guided companion for *The Connection Experience*, providing space to record thoughts, quotes, and affirmations to support your journey towards greater self-awareness and connection.

The Connection Cleanse
A transformative experience designed to help you clear negative energy from your life and create space for positive, high-vibrational connections. Through a combination of self-reflection, guided exercises, and energy work, you can release what no longer serves you and open up to the possibilities of what could be.

The Connection Cleanse Toolkit
A powerful resource designed to help you cleanse and revitalize your energy. It contains a variety of tools and exercises that can help you disconnect from draining connections, and attract positive and uplifting energy into your life.

One Minute Manifest e-Mini
By taking just one minute to focus your energy and attention on your goals, you can start to attract the experiences you desire into your life. This practice aligns with the teachings of *The Connection Experience*, which emphasizes the power of connection and awareness in creating a fulfilling life.

Be Your Own Cheerleader e-Mini
Helps you tap into the power of self-belief and positivity to create affirmations that inspire and motivate you to achieve your goals. By infusing your affirmations with positive energy, you can cheer yourself on and accomplish anything you set your mind to.

About Tricia

Tricia was born in Toronto, Canada and resides in the Cayman Islands. Her passion for helping drives her to write, speak, and mentor others seeking joy, freedom, and unshakable personal power through Gratitude, Connection, and Action.

Being a HeartMath® Certified Trainer, a published author, and TEDx speaker, Tricia shares her inspiring and honest vulnerabilities to encourage her readers to be strong. She truly believes that navigating through valuable life lessons, brings new perspectives that invite readers to connect to their heart and live an authentic and fulfilling life. She has had many of her own opportunities to navigate life challenges with careers, parenthood, living abroad, adversities, as well as healing, and embracing life to the fullest.

"What truly matters, is how we experience our stories within the world around us. I invite you to step into the flow of Gratitude, Connection, Action to create a field of opportunity for positive change in your life."

Tricia Sybersma

Join the community to stay up to date on the newest books, e-minis, gifts and other offerings.

Email:

Tricia@TriciaSybersma.com

Website:

www.TriciaSybersma.com

Facebook:

/Ggnow2015

Instagram:

/triciasybersma

Twitter:

/tsybersma1

RedBubble:

/Tsybersma

The Gratitude Experience is a powerful and inspiring book that will transform your life by teaching you how to cultivate gratitude in a mindful way.

Learn how to shift your perspective and focus on the positive aspects of your life, even in the face of challenges and difficulties. By practicing gratitude, you'll open yourself up to new opportunities and experiences, and you'll start to see the world in a more positive light.

Start your journey of gratitude today and experience the transformative power of this life-changing practice.

WHAT PEOPLE ARE SAYING

"The biggest thing I've learned about is why it's so important to pay attention to how we're feeling. That paying attention to our feelings, which are in our hearts, is the quickest way to restore connection to our heart energy.

The "aha" moment here was understanding that that is why feelings are so powerful. If our heart energy is what is creating our lives, by accessing the feelings in our hearts, we're tapping directly into the energy that's creating our lives. I'll be going through the book again and again I think."

~ Dawn

"Realizing the vast spectrum of connections that are not only within the world, but within our selves was a huge shifting piece for me. Now I can start to understand why I feel so sensitive at times, and feel empowered to make a conscious choice about what I am willing to connect to, or not! So eye-opening!"

~ Nathan

"In my ever-continuing path towards alignment, this book comes at a perfect time, another tool that brings tremendous benefit along with a deep understanding. Helping me level deeper and deeper into my learning."

~ Renato

Find It

A

Affirmation - definition **60**
Astrology - definition **51**
Astronomy - definition **51**

B

Benefits of connecting to your Inner Power **36**

C

Coherence - definition **18**
Community and beyond **47**
Community - definition **47**
Compass **56**
Connecting to your Unique Perspective (UP) **25**
Connection between Inner Power and ego **35**
Connection between our UP and Inner Power **35**
Connection - definition **9**
Connection Influences **12**
Connections to you **14**
Connection to nature **43**
Connection to the world around you **42**
Connection to your energy **19**
Connection to your Inner Power **34**
Connection to your physical body **16**

D

Destination - definition **57**
Destinations **57**
Difference between fitting in and Connection **48**
Difference between manifesting & destination **58**

E

Ego - definition **36**
Emotion - definition **20**

F

Feel - definition **20**
Feeling - definition **20**
Feelings, emotions, and thoughts **20**
Field of Connection **10**
Filtering information **27**

G

Getting in the Connection vibe **12**
Gratitude Experience **7**

H

Heart Intelligence **23**
Heart intelligence - definition **23**

I

Imagination and Intuition **30**
Imagination - definition **31**
Intro to navigating **55**
Intuition - definition **30**

M

Manifest - definition **38**

N

Nature - definition **44**
Navigate - definition **55**

O

One Minute Manifest **39**

P

Patterns **52**
Perspective - definition **27**
Planning your next destination - checklist **59**
Plugging into feelings **22**
Power - definition **34**

Q

Quick Coherence Technique **18**

R

Restore Connection to communities & beyond **53**
Restore Connection to energy **24**
Restore Connection to nature **45**
Restore Connection to your Inner Power **37**
Restore Connection to your physical body **17**
Restore Connection to your 'UP' **31**

S

Self - definition **36**

T

The Connection Experience **13**
Thought - definition **20**

U

Unique - definition **26**

W

What is community **47**
What is Connection **9**
What is nature **43**
What is Unique Perspective **26**
Working with your 'UP' **29**

Connection